the changing Seasons

Johann-Bernard Klombbek (19th Century) *The Timber Cart in Winter*

Grange
BOOKS

Helen Allingham (1848-1926) *Gathering Bluebells*

the changing Seasons

Compiled By Anna Nicholas

Pierre-Georges Dieterle (1844-1937) *The Harvest*

A selection of poems and quotations

The Publishers would like to acknowledge the following for permission to reproduce copyright material:
Page 34 and 35, The Society of Authors, representatives for the estate of Walter de la Mare for 'Here Am I, a Poor Old Guy' and 'Brueghel's Winter' by Walter de la Mare; Page 38, Laurence Pollinger and Little, Brown & Co for 'Christmas Reunion' by Peter de Vries (from The Tents of Wickedness; the poem originally appeared in The New Yorker).

The Publishers have made every effort to trace copyright material reproduced within this compilation. If, however, they have inadvertently made any error they would be grateful for notification.

Many thanks to Paperchase, London for kindly allowing us to use their papers.

Pictures courtesy of The Bridgeman Art Library.

Ernest Arthur Rowe (1862-1922) Loseley Park, Surrey

Pictures courtesy of The Bridgeman Art Library

Published in 1995 by Grange Books
An imprint of Grange Books PLC
The Grange, Grange Yard
London SE1 3AG

Copyright © 1994 Regency House Publishing Limited

ISBN 1 85627 621 X

Printed in Italy

Pierre Auguste Renoir (1841-1919) *Spring at Châtou*

six

Der spring is sprung,

Der grass is riz,

I wonder where dem boidies is?

Der little boids is on der wing,

Ain't dat absoid?

Der little wings is on der boid!

Spring in New York. Anon.

The year's at the spring,

The day's at the morn;

Morning's at seven;

The hillside's dew-pearl'd;

The lark's on the wing;

The snail's on the thorn;

God's in His heaven —

All's right with the world!

From: *Pippa's Song*. Robert Browning 1812-1889

Fred Hines (fl.1896) *In Blossom Time*

To every thing there is a season, and a time to every purpose under the heaven.

Proverbs 3, 1

Spring, the sweet spring, is the year's pleasant king;
Then blooms each thing, then maids dance in a ring,
Cold doth not sting, the pretty birds do sing:
Cuckoo, jug-jug, pu-we, to-witta-woo!

The palm and may make country houses gay,
Lambs frisk and play, the shepherds pipe all day,
And we hear aye birds tune this merry lay:
Cuckoo, jug-jug, pu-we, to-witta-woo!

The fields breathe sweet, the daisies kiss our feet,
Young lovers meet, old wives a-sunning sit;
In every street these tunes our ears do greet:
Cuckoo, jug-jug, pu-we, to-witta-woo!
Spring, the sweet spring!

Thomas Nash 1567-1601

I heard a thousand blended notes
While in a grove I sate reclined,
In that sweet mood when pleasant thoughts
Bring sad thoughts to the mind.

To her fair works did Nature link
The human soul that through me ran;
And much it grieved my heart to think
What Man has made of Man.

Through primrose tufts, in that sweet bower,
The periwinkle trail'd its wreaths;
And 'tis my faith that every flower
Enjoys the air it breathes.

The birds around me hopp'd and play'd,
Their thoughts I cannot measure, –
But the least motion which they made
It seem'd a thrill of pleasure.

The budding twigs spread out their fan
To catch the breezy air;
And I must think, do all I can,
That there was pleasure there.

If this belief from heaven be sent,
If such be Nature's holy plan,
Have I not reason to lament
What Man has made of Man?

Written in Early Spring.
William Wordsworth 1770-1850

Beatrice Parsons (1870-1955) *Spring Woods, Gravetye, Sussex*

t e n

O, to be in England

Now that April's there,

And whoever wakes in England

Sees, some morning, unaware,

That the lowest boughs and the brushwood sheaf

Round the elm-tree bole are in tiny leaf,

While the chaffinch sings on the orchard bough

In England – now!

And after April, when May follows,

And the whitethroat builds, and all the swallows!

Hark, where my blossom'd pear-tree in the hedge

Leans to the field and scatters on the clover

Blossoms and dewdrops – at the bent spray's edge –

That's the wise thrush; he sings each song twice over,

Lest you should think he never could recapture

The first fine careless rapture!

And though the fields look rough with hoary dew,

All will be gay when noontide wakes anew

The buttercups, the little children's dower

– Far brighter than this gaudy melon-flower!

Robert Browning 1812-1889

eleven

If the oak is out before the ash,

Then we are going to have a splash,

But if the ash is out before the oak,

Summer will be just one long soak.

Alfred Glendening (1861-1903) *Spring Flowers*

Sir Edward Burne-Jones (1833-1898) *The March Marigold*

No need for confusion if we but recall
That Easter on the first Sunday after the full moon
following the vernal equinox doth fall.

Rhyme for remembering the date of Easter. Justin Richardson

thirteen

The silver birch is a dainty lady,
　　She wears a satin gown;
　The elm-tree makes the churchyard shady,
　　She will not live in town.

The English oak is a sturdy fellow;
　　He gets his green coat late;
The willow is smart in a coat of yellow,
　　While brown the beech trees wait.

Such a gay green gown God gives the larches –
　　As green as He is good!
The hazels hold up their arms for arches
　　When Spring rides through the wood.

The chestnut's proud, and the lilac's pretty,
　　The poplar's gentle and tall,
But the plane tree's kind to the poor dull city –
　　I love him best of all!

E. Nesbit 1858-1924

Don't say that spring has come until you can put your foot on nine daisies.

Old English Proverb

George Henry Boughton (1833-1905) *Springtime*

Most glorious Lord of Lyfe! that, on this day,
  Didst make Thy triumph over death and sin;
  And, having harrowd hell, didst bring away
  Captivity thence captive, us to win:
This joyous day, deare Lord, with joy begin;
And grant that we, for whom Thou diddest dye,
Being with Thy deare blood clene washt from sin,
May live for ever in felicity!
And that Thy love we weighing worthily,
May likewise love Thee for the same againe;
And for Thy sake, that all lyke deare didst buy,
With love may one another entertayne!
  So let us love, deare Love, lyke as we ought,
  – Love is the lesson which the Lord us taught.

Easter. Edmund Spenser 1552-1599

Henry John Yeend King (1855-1924) *Girls Collecting Flowers*

When daisies pied and violets blue,
  And lady-smocks all silver-white,
And cuckoo-buds of yellow hue
  Do paint the meadows with delight,
The cuckoo then, on every tree,
  Mocks married men; for thus sings he,
          Cuckoo!
Cuckoo, cuckoo! – O word of fear,
Unpleasing to a married ear!

When shepherds pipe on oaten straws,
  And merry larks are ploughmen's clocks,
When turtles tread, and rooks, and daws,
  And maidens bleach their summer smocks
The cuckoo then, on every tree,
Mocks married men; for thus sings he,
          Cuckoo!
Cuckoo, cuckoo! – O word of fear,
Unpleasing to a married ear!

William Shakespeare 1564-1616

One
swallow
does not
make a
summer.

Greek Proverb

Sir Hubert von Herkomer (1849-1914) *In the Garden*

St Swithin's Day, if thou be fair,
For forty days 'twill rain no more,
St Swithin's day, if thou bring rain,
For forty days it will remain.

Pierre Auguste Renoir (1841-1919) *Umbrellas*

nineteen

*A leaky
May and
a June,
Brings on
the harvest
very soon.*

Vincent van Gogh (1853-1890) *Noon (after Millet) La Méridienne*

A swarm of bees in May,

Is worth a load of hay,

A swarm of bees in June

Is worth a silver spoon,

But a swarm in July,

Is not worth a fly.

HE WHO BATHES IN MAY,

WILL SOON BE LAID TO CLAY;

HE WHO BATHES IN JUNE

WILL SING A MERRY TUNE;

HE WHO BATHES IN JULY,

MUST DANCE TILL HE IS DRY.

Ernst Meilsner (19th century) *Mother and Child by a Duck Pond*

*The Queen of Hearts
She made some tarts
All on a summer's day;
The Knave of Hearts
He stole the tarts,
And took them clean away.*

The European Magazine, April 1782

twenty-three

When as the rye reach to the chin,
  And chopcherry, chopcherry ripe within,
Strawberries swimming in the cream,
And school-boys playing in the stream;
  Then O, then O, then O my true love said,
    Till that time come again,
She could not live a maid.

A Summer Song. George Peele 1558?-1597

Joshua Cristall (1767-1847) *The Gleaners*

twenty-four

Henry Sutton Palmer (1854-1933) *The Cottar's Pride – A Cottage Garden*

'Tis the last rose of summer
Left blooming alone;
All her lovely companions
Are faded and gone.

Thomas Moore 1779-1852

twenty-five

Sumer is icumen in,
  Lhude sing cuccu!
Groweth sed, and bloweth med,
  And springeth the wude nu –
    Sing cuccu!

Awe bleteth after lomb,
  Lhouth after calve cu;
Bulluc sterteth, bucke verteth,
  Murie sing Cuccu!

Cuccu, cuccu, well singes thu, cuccu:
  Ne swike thu naver nu;
Sing cuccu, nu, sing cuccu,
  Sing cuccu, sing cuccu, nu!

Anon. c. 1226

lhude) loud.
awe) ewe.
lhouth) loweth.
sterteth) leaps.
swike) cease.

F. Sydney Muschamp (fl. 1870-1903) *Feeding the Doves*

Alfred John Billinghurst (b.1880) *The Herbaceous Border*

twenty-seven

Let the wealthy and great,

Roll in splendour and state,

I envy them not I declare it.

I eat my own lamb, my own chicken and ham,

I sheer my own fleece, and I wear it.

I have fruit, I have flowers,

I have lawns, I have bowers,

The lark is my morning alarming.

So jolly boys now,

Here's God-speed to the plough,

Long life and success to all farming.

Old Harvest Rhyme

Thomas Blinks (fl.c. 1880) *Harvest Scene*

Frederick Morgan (1856-1927) *The Apple Gatherers*

Autumn steals summer like a thief.

twenty-nine

*I*n brisk wind of September

The heavy-headed fruits

Shake upon their bending boughs

And drop from the golden shoots;

Some glow golden in the sun,

Some show green and streaked,

Some set forth a purple bloom,

Some blush rosy-cheeked.

From: *A Year's Windfalls.* Christina Rossetti 1830-1894

Sir James Dromgole Linton (1840-1916) *Thanksgiving*

Alexander Demetrius Goltz (b.1857) *Autumn Roses*

Season of mists and mellow fruitfulness,
Close bosom-friend of the maturing sun;
Conspiring with him how to load and bless
With fruit the vines that round the thatch-eaves run;
To bend with apples the moss'd cottage-trees,
And fill all fruit with ripeness to the core;
To swell the gourd, and plump the hazel shells
With a sweet kernel; to set budding more,
And still more, later flowers for the bees,
Until they think warm days will never cease;
For Summer has o'erbrimmed their clammy cells.

Who hath not seen thee oft amid thy store?
Sometimes whoever seeks abroad may find
Thee sitting careless on a granary floor,
Thy hair soft-lifted by the winnowing wind;
Or on a half-reap'd furrow fast asleep,
Drowsed with the fume of poppies, while thy hook
Spares the next swath and all its twined flowers;
And sometimes like a gleaner thou dost keep
Steady thy laden head across a brook;
Or by a cider-press, with patient look,
Thou watchest the last oozings, hours by hours.

Where are the songs of Spring? Ay, where are they?
Think not of them, thou hast thy music too,
While barred clouds bloom the soft-dying day
And touch the stubble-plains with rosy hue;
Then in a wailful choir the small gnats mourn
Among the river-sallows, borne aloft
Or sinking as the light wind lives or dies;
And full-grown lambs bleat from hilly bourn;
Hedge-crickets sing, and now with treble soft
The redbreast whistles from a garden-croft;
And gathering swallows twitter in the skies.

Ode to Autumn. John Keats 1795-1821

Lexden L. Pocock (1875-1914) *Girl and Beehives*

When Autumn bleak and sunburnt do appear,
  With his gold hand gilding the falling leaf,
Bringing up Winter to fulfil the year,
  Bearing upon his back the ripèd sheaf,
When all the hills with woody seed is white,
When levin[1]-fires and lemes[2] do meet from far the sight;
  When the fair apple, red as even sky,
    Do bend the tree unto the fruitful ground.
  When juicy pears, and berries of black dye,
    Do dance in air, and call the eyes around:
Then, be the even foul, or even fair,
Methinks my hartys joy is steyncèd[3] with some care.

1. lightning   2. gleams   3. mingled

Thomas Chatterton 1752-1770

t h i r t y - t w o

A fair October and a good blast, will
blow the hag and her broom away fast...

Old English Proverb

William Holman Hunt (1827-1910) *Our English Coasts (Strayed Sheep)*

Sir John Everett Millais (1826-1896) *Autumn Leaves*

Here am I,
A poor old Guy:
Legs in a bonfire,
Head in the sky:

Shoeless my toes,
Wild stars behind,
Smoke in my nose,
And my eye-peeps blind;

Old hat, old straw -
In this disgrace;
While the wildfire gleams
On a mask for face.

Ay, all I am made of
Only trash is;
And soon – soon,
Will be dust and ashes.

Walter de la Mare 1873-1956

thirty-four

Pieter Brueghel the Younger (c.1564-1638) *Winter*

Jagg'd mountain peaks and skies ice-green
Wall in the wild cold scene below.
Churches, farms, bare copse, the sea
In freezing quiet of winter show;
Where ink-black shapes on fields in flood
Curling, skating, and sliding go.
To left, a gabled tavern; a blaze;
Peasants; a watching child; and lo,
Muffled, mute – beneath naked trees
In sharp perspective set a-row –
Trudge huntsmen, sinister spears aslant,
Dogs snuffing behind them in the snow;
And arrowlike, lean, athwart the air
Swoops into space a crow.

But flame, nor ice, nor piercing rock,
Nor silence, as of a frozen sea,
Nor that slant inward infinite line
Of signboard, bird, and hill, and tree.
Give more than subtle hint of him
Who squandered here life's mystery.

From: *Brueghel's Winter*. Walter de la Mare 1873-1956

thirty-five

It was not in Winter
Our loving lot was cast;
It was the Time of Roses, –
We pluck'd them as we pass'd;

That churlish season never frown'd
    On early lovers yet: –
Oh, no – the world was newly crown'd
    With flowers when first we met!

'Twas twilight, and I bade you go,
    But still you held me fast;
It was the Time of Roses, –
    We pluck'd them as we passed. –

What else could peer thy glowing cheek
    That tears began to stud!
And when I ask'd the like of Love,
    You snatched a damask bud;

And oped it to the dainty core,
    Still glowing to the last, –
It was the Time of Roses, –
    We pluck'd them as we pass'd!

Thomas Hood 1799-1845

Nils Hans Christiansen (late 19th century) *A Stag in a Wooded Winter Landscape*

Now winter nights enlarge
  The number of their hours,
And clouds their storms discharge
  Upon the airy towers.
Now let the chimneys blaze
  And cups o'erflow with wine;
Let well-tuned words amaze
  With harmony divine.
Now yellow waxen lights
  Shall wait on honey love,
While youthful revels, masques, and courtly sights
  Sleep's leaden spells remove.

This time doth well dispense
  With lovers' long discourse;
Much speech hath some defence,
  Though beauty no remorse.
All do not all things well;
  Some measures comely tread,
Some knotted riddles tell,
  Some poems smoothly read.
The summer hath his joys,
  And winter his delights;
Though love and all his pleasures are but toys,
  They shorten tedious nights.

Thomas Campion 1567?-1619

Viggo Johansen (1851-1935) *Happy Christmas*

Since last the tutelary hearth
  Has seen the bursting pod of kin,
I've thought how good the family mould,
  How solid and how genuine.

Now once again the aunts are here,
  The uncles, sisters, brothers,
With candy in the children's hair,
  The grownups in each other's.

There's talk of saving room for pie;
  Grandma discusses her neuralgia.
I long for time to pass, so I
  Can think of all this with nostalgia.

Christmas Family Reunion. Peter de Vries b. 1910

When icicles hang by the wall
  And Dick the shepherd blows his nail,
And Tom bears logs into the hall,
  And milk comes frozen home in pail;
When blood is nippt, and ways be foul,
Then nightly sings the staring owl
            Too-whoo!
Too-whit, too-whoo! A merry note!
While greasy Joan doth keel the pot.

When all about the wind doth blow,
  And coughing drowns the parson's saw,
And birds sit brooding in the snow,
  And Marian's nose looks red and raw;
When roasted crabs hiss in the bowl —
Then nightly sings the staring owl
            Too-whoo!
To-whit, To-whoo! A merry note!
While greasy Joan doth keel the pot.

William Shakespeare 1564-1616

Alois Arnegger (fl.1900) *Hocheisgruppe, Austria*

t h i r t y - n i n e

If Candlemas Day be warm and bright,
Winter will take another bite,
But if Candlemas Day brings cold and rain,
Winter is gone, and won't come again.

Camille Pissarro (1831-1903) *White Frost*

A. Bredou (19th century) *Figures by a River Before a Watermill*

*Western wind, when will thou blow
The small rain down can rain?
Christ, if my love were in my arms
And I in my bed again!*

The Lover in Winter Plaineth for the Spring. Anon. 16th century

In a drear-nighted December,
  Too happy, happy tree,
Thy branches ne'er remember
  Their green felicity:
The north cannot undo them,
With a sleety whistle through them;
Nor frozen thawings glue them
  From budding at the prime.

In a drear-nighted December,
  Too happy, happy brook,
Thy bubblings ne'er remember
  Apollo's summer look;
But with a sweet forgetting,
They stay their crystal fretting,
Never, never petting
  About the frozen time.

Ah! would 'twere so with many
  A gentle girl and boy!
But were there ever any
  Writhed not at passed joy?
To know the change and feel it,
When there is none to heal it,
Nor numbed sense to steal it,
  Was never said in rhyme.

John Keats 1795-1821

Richardo Diaque (19th century) *A Winter's Walk*

forty-two

Bread and milk for breakfast,
And woollen frocks to wear,
And a crumb for robin redbreast
On the cold days of the year.

Christina Rossetti 1830-1894

Edward Algernon Stuart Douglas (b.1850-fl.1918) *On the Scent*

The north wind doth blow and we shall have snow,

And what will the robin do then, poor thing?

He'll sit in the barn and keep himself warm

And hide his head under his wing, poor thing!

The north wind doth blow and we shall have snow,

And what will the swallow do then, poor thing?

Oh, do you not know? He's gone long ago

To a land that is warmer than ours, poor thing!

The north wind doth blow and we shall have snow,

And what will the children do then, poor things?

When lessons are done they'll jump, skip and run,

And play till they make themselves warm, poor things.

Old Rhyme

Mary Ensor (fl.1871-1874) *Winter (Roundel with Robin)*

Joseph Farquharson (1846-1935) *The Sun had Closed the Winter's Day*

Blow, blow, thou winter wind,

Thou art not so unkind

  As man's ingratitude;

Thy tooth is not so keen,

Because thou art not seen,

  Although thy breath be rude.

Heigh ho! sing, heigh ho! unto the green holly:

Most friendship is feigning, most loving mere folly:

  Then heigh ho, the holly!

  This life is most jolly.

Freeze, freeze, thou bitter sky,

That dost not bite so nigh

  As benefits forgot:

Though thou the waters warp,

Thy sting is not so sharp

  As friend remember'd not.

Heigh ho! sing, heigh ho! unto the green holly:

Most friendship is feigning, most loving mere folly:

  Then heigh ho, the holly!

  This life is most jolly.

William Shakespeare 1564-1616

forty-five

Four Seasons fill the measure of the year;
There are four seasons in the mind of Man:
He has his lusty Spring, when fancy clear
Takes in all beauty with an easy span:

He has his Summer, when luxuriously
Spring's honey'd cud of youthful thought he loves
To ruminate, and by such dreaming high
Is nearest unto heaven: quiet coves

His soul has in its Autumn, when his wings
He furleth close; contented so to look
On mists in idleness – to let fair things
Pass by unheeded as a threshold brook: –

He has his Winter too of pale misfeature,
Or else he would forego his mortal nature.

The Human Seasons. John Keats 1795-1821

Robert Henri (1865-1929) *New York Street Under the Snow*

Frederick Daniel Hardy (1826-1911) *Christmas Visitors*

O World! O Life! O Time!
On whose last steps I climb,
    Trembling at that where I had stood before;
When will return the glory of your prime?
    No more — O never more!

Out of the day and night
A joy has taken flight:
    Fresh spring, and summer, and winter hoar
Move my faint heart with grief, but with delight
    No more — O never more!

A Lament. Percy Bysshe Shelley 1792-1822

forty-seven

Thirty days hath September,
April, June, and November;
All the rest have thirty-one,
Excepting February alone
And that has twenty-eight days clear
And twenty-nine in each leap year.